It's another Quality Book from CGP

This book is for 6-7 year olds.

Whatever subject you're doing it's the same old story — there are lots of facts and you've just got to learn them. KS1 English is no different.

Happily this CGP book gives you all that important information as clearly and concisely as possible.

It's also got some daft bits in to try and make the whole experience at least vaguely entertaining for you.

What CGP is all about

Our sole aim here at CGP is to produce the highest quality books — carefully written, immaculately presented and dangerously close to being funny.

Then we work our socks off to get them out to you — at the cheapest possible prices.

CONTENTS

SECTION ONE — SPELLING

Writing Clearly 1
Spelling Vowel Sounds 2
Word Endings 4
Longer Words 6

SECTION TWO — READING COMPREHENSION

Reading Carefully 8
Answering the Questions 10
Answering the Questions 12
Answering the Questions 14
Saying What You Think 16
Practice Reading Comprehension 18

SECTION THREE — WRITING SKILLS

Starting and Ending Sentences 20
Questions and Exclamations 22
Don't Use 'and' Too Much 24
Use Interesting Words 26
Write In Clear Sentences 28
Speech Marks 30

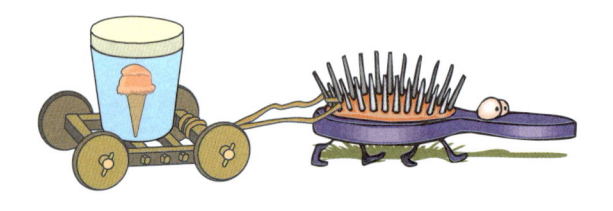

Section Four — Writing Stories

Planning a Story	32
Starting a Story	34
Using Describing Words	36
Using Different Words	38
Ending a Story	40
You Write a Story	42

Section Five — Other Writing

Titles and Introductions	44
Sub-headings	46
Bullet Points	48
Looking for Facts	50
Endings	52
Practice Writing Exercise	54
Writing a Letter	56
Answers	58

Published by Coordination Group Publications Ltd.

Contributors:
Simon Cook
Taissa Csáky
Gemma Hallam
Iain Nash

With thanks to Mr Tansley, Mr Nicol and Class 2 at Broughton-in-Furness Primary School.

ISBN: 978 1 84146 182 3

Groovy website: www.cgpbooks.co.uk

Jolly bits of clipart from CorelDRAW®

Printed by Elanders Hindson Ltd, Newcastle upon Tyne.

Text, design, layout and original illustrations © Coordination Group Publications Ltd. 2000
All rights reserved.

SPELLING

Writing Clearly

Take care! If you don't write clearly, no one can tell if your spellings are right.

a ✓   u ✗

This 'a' looks great.   Yuck. This 'a' looks like a 'u'.

Q1 Copy these letters.

a   b   d   e

a   ....

k   l   p   q

....

t   u   v   y

....

Don't let your letters get mixed up.

Q2 Copy these letter joins.

ai   ar   ul   ou   un

ai   ....

Keep it neat...
Don't let different letters get jumbled up.

Section One — Spelling

Spelling Vowel Sounds

Watch out — there are different ways to spell some vowel sounds.

stree**t**   **st**ea**m**

These bits sound the same.

Q1 Join up the words with the same vowel sound.

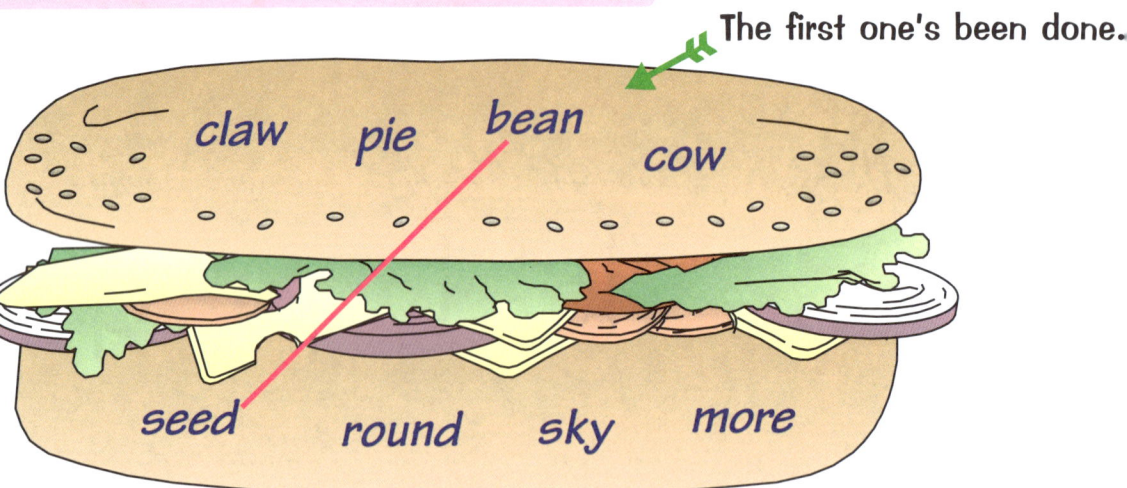

The first one's been done.

claw   pie   bean   cow

seed   round   sky   more

The same sound can have different spellings.

Q2 Put a circle round the words in each list with the same vowel sound as the first word.

The 'oa' bit sounds like the 'o' in slow and go.

① boat   (slow,) boy, cow, (go)

② train   plate, cat, play, park

③ said   reach, red, bread, feet

④ round   show, how, good, sound

Section One — Spelling

Q3 Choose the **right spelling** to help you **fill in** these words.

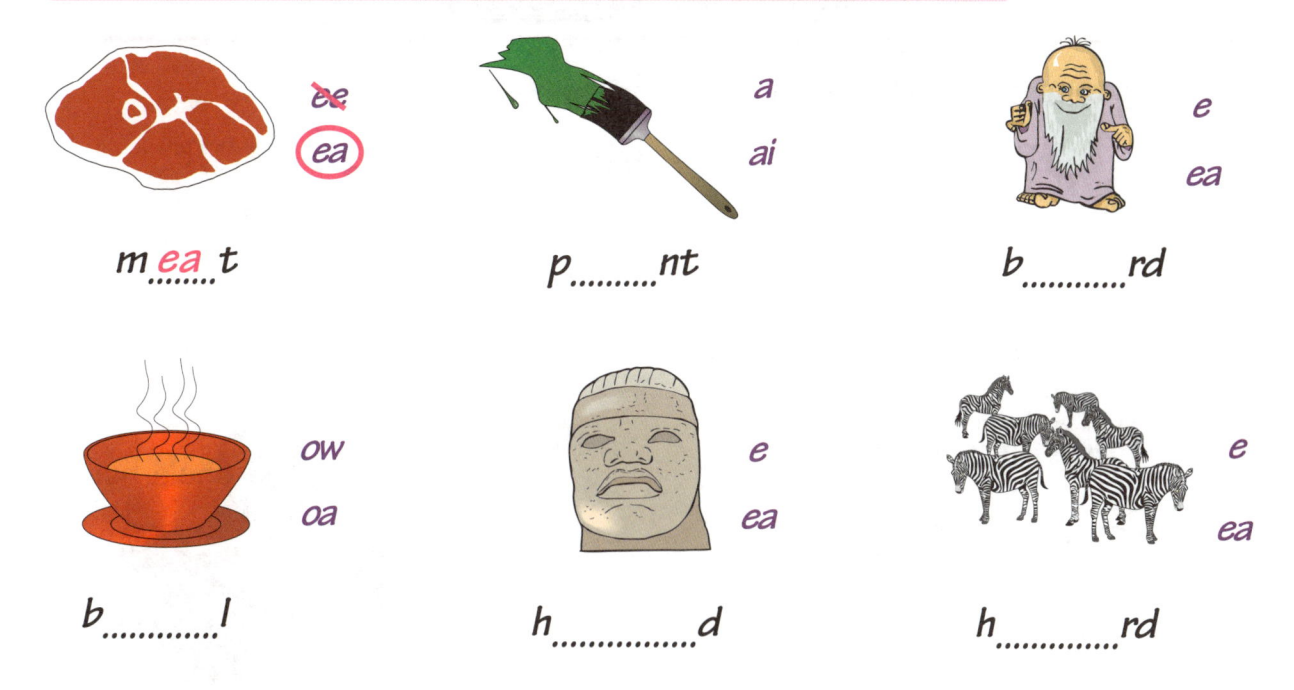

~~ee~~
(ea)

m_ea_t

a
ai

p_____nt

e
ea

b_____rd

ow
oa

b_____l

e
ea

h_____d

e
ea

h_____rd

Don't miss any letters out.

Q4 All these words have a letter **missing**. Write each one out **properly**.

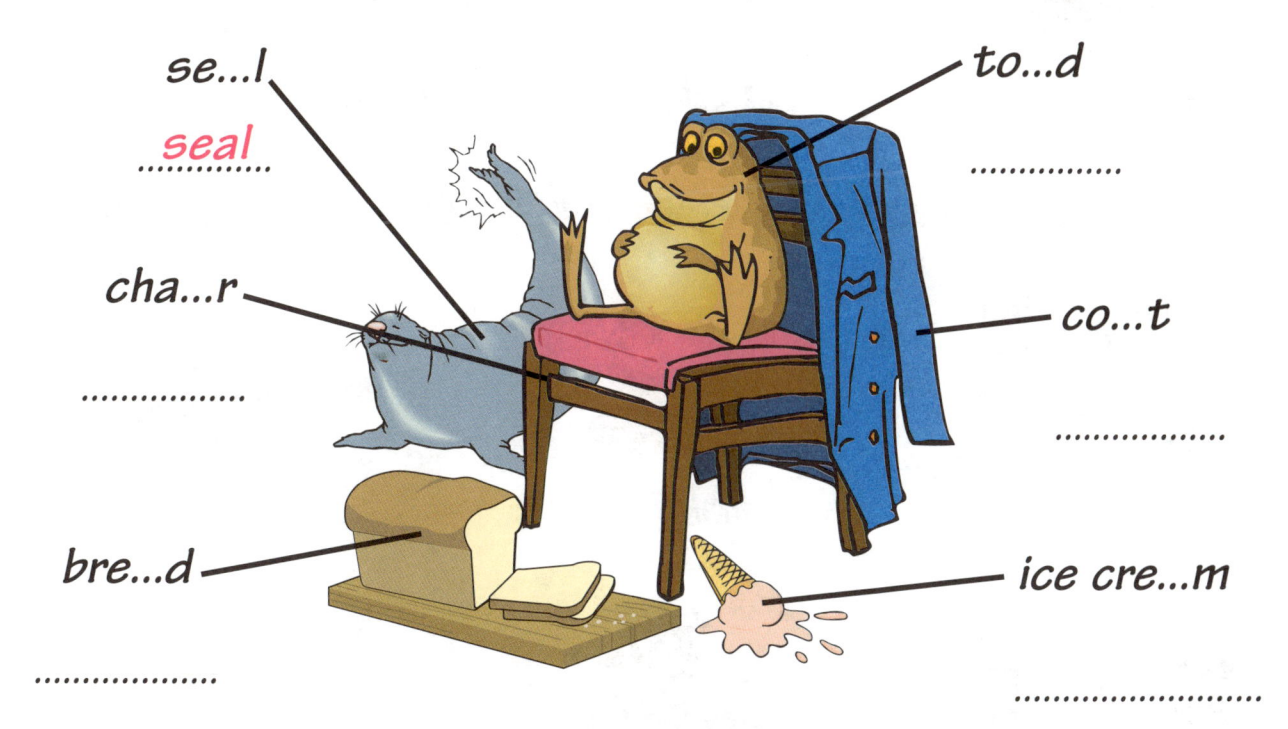

se...l
seal

cha...r
....

bre...d
....

to...d
....

co...t
....

ice cre...m
....

Get your spellings just right...
The same sound can be spelt **different ways**.

Section One — Spelling

Word Endings

The <u>endings</u> of words can be really hard to spell.

pear   **share**   **hair**

These endings all sound the <u>same</u>.

Be careful — some words have an 'e' on the end that you <u>can't</u> hear, like shar**e**.

Q1 Underline **all** the words with an 'e' on the end.

I'm reading a fairy tale.

Mrs Witch made a horrible face.

Have a bite of this nice apple.

<u>Don't</u> leave the 'e' out when you write.

cake   **drive**

Q2 These words are **missing** a letter 'e'. Add it on to give the right spellings.

lat**e**....   snak....   hol...

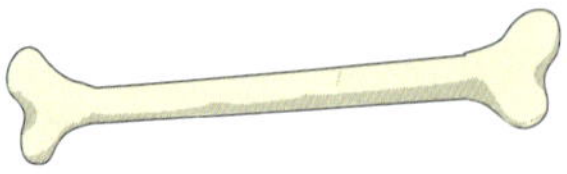

gat....   shar....   bon....

Section One — Spelling

Q3 Join the words with the **same ending sound**. Don't forget they're **spelt differently**.

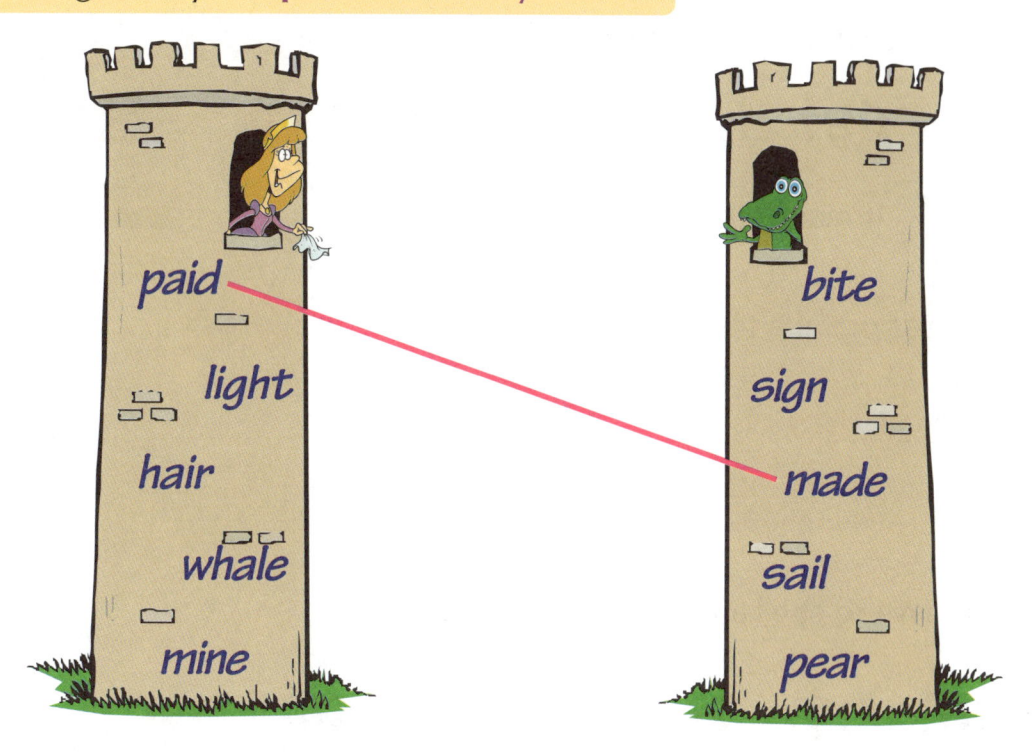

Left tower: paid, light, hair, whale, mine
Right tower: bite, sign, made, sail, pear

(paid — made connected)

Q4 Use the endings in the blue box to **fill in** the words around the picture.

Blue box: -ail, ~~-ight~~, ~~-ign~~, ~~-are~~, ~~-ace~~, -ight, -ale, -ear, -ple, -ail

- a squ*are* s*ign*
- a p......... f*ace*
- p...........
- pur..........
- sn............
- m............
- a br*ight* l............

Learn your word endings...
Watch out for 'e's you <u>can't hear</u>.

Section One — Spelling

Longer Words

You can split long words into shorter bits.

for + get + ful = forgetful

It makes them a lot easier to spell.

Q1 Add these short bits together to make new **long words**.

in + side = *inside*   birth + day = ...

be + fore = ...   care + ful = ...

When you have to spell a long word, don't worry.

container ➤ con + tai + ner

Work out the spelling of each bit, just like you would for a short word.

Always spell long words one bit at a time.

Q2 Fill in the **correct missing bit** in each word.

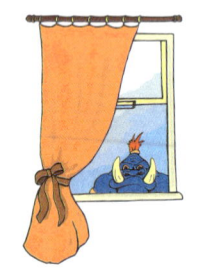

win + dow/~~do~~ = win *dow*

fa + mi/ma + ly = fa..........ly

com + plane/plain = com............

ho + la/li + day = ho..........day

Section One — Spelling

Q3 Choose the right bit to fill in each word sum.

sur / su + prise = **surprise**

sum / some + times = ...

ce / care + ful = ...

rea / ree + ching = ...

slow / slo + ly = ...

fo / for + get + ting = ...

Q4 Fill in these word sums.

Use the pictures to help you.

un + der + **neath** = ...

bas + **ket** = ...

.... + day = ...

Q5 **Learn** these words, then **cover them up** and write them out.

cleaning   although   surprised

because   careful   happiness

Break long words into bits...

You've got to spell them out <u>one bit at a time</u>.

Section One — Spelling

Reading Carefully

In the comprehension test every page has a bit of writing and some questions.

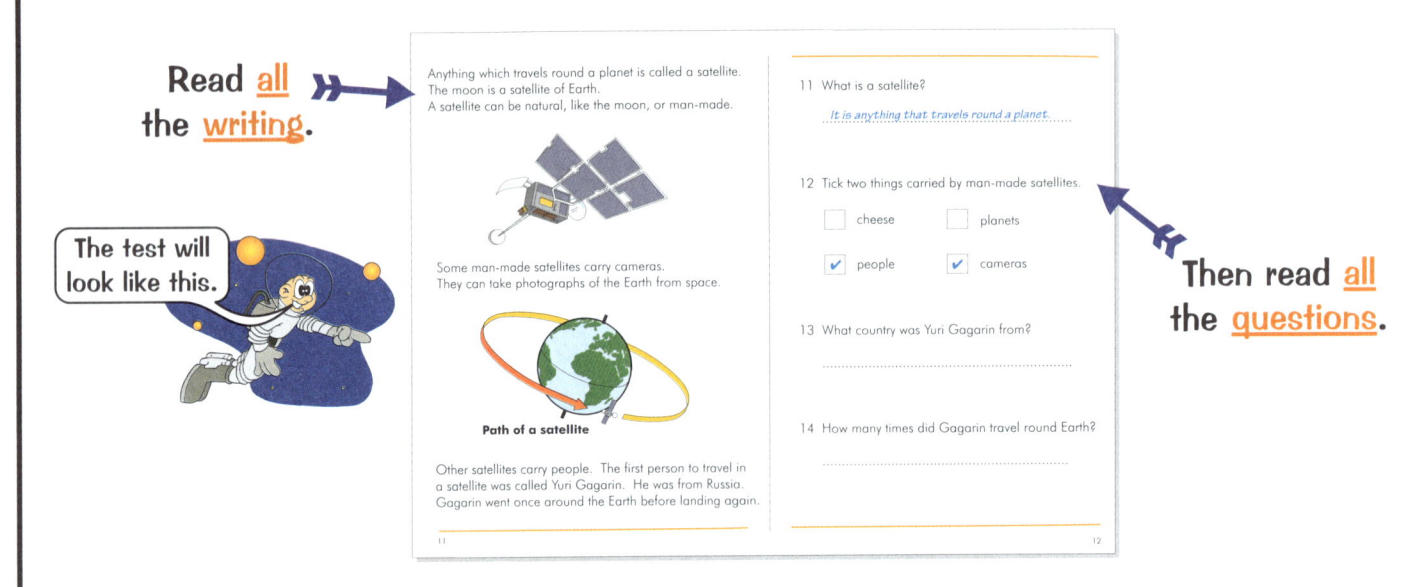

Read **all** the writing. →

The test will look like this.

Sample test page showing:
- Anything which travels round a planet is called a satellite. The moon is a satellite of Earth. A satellite can be natural, like the moon, or man-made.
- Some man-made satellites carry cameras. They can take photographs of the Earth from space.
- **Path of a satellite**
- Other satellites carry people. The first person to travel in a satellite was called Yuri Gagarin. He was from Russia. Gagarin went once around the Earth before landing again.

Questions:
11. What is a satellite?
    It is anything that travels round a planet.
12. Tick two things carried by man-made satellites.
    ☐ cheese   ☐ planets
    ☑ people   ☑ cameras
13. What country was Yuri Gagarin from?
14. How many times did Gagarin travel round Earth?

← Then read **all** the questions.

Read everything properly **before** you answer the questions.

Q1 Read the **writing** and the **questions**. Then **answer** the questions.

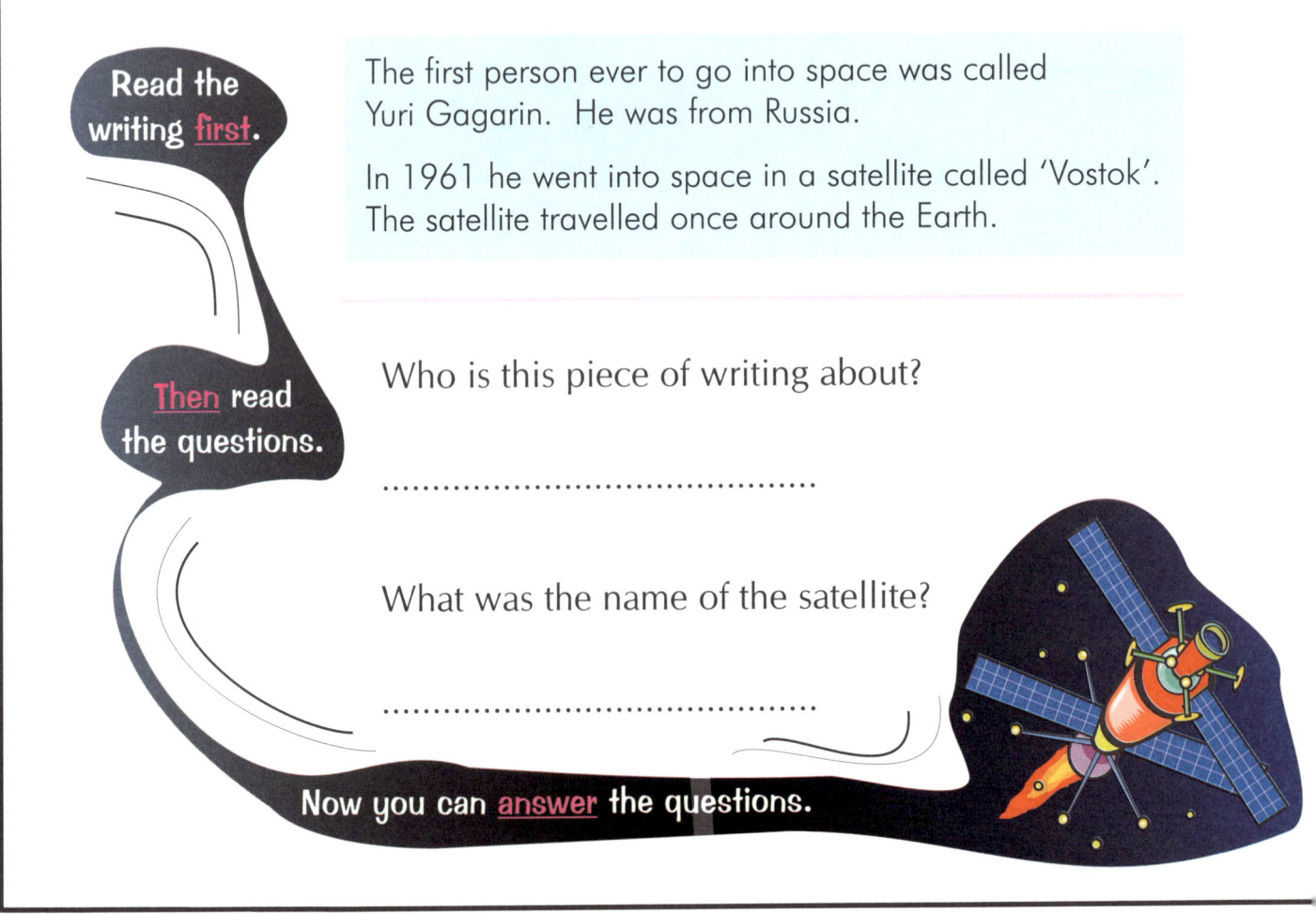

Read the writing first.

> The first person ever to go into space was called Yuri Gagarin. He was from Russia.
>
> In 1961 he went into space in a satellite called 'Vostok'. The satellite travelled once around the Earth.

Then read the questions.

Who is this piece of writing about?

....

What was the name of the satellite?

....

Now you can **answer** the questions.

Section Two — Reading Comprehension

Read every word on the page carefully.

Q2 Read the writing and the questions. Then **answer** the questions.

Kirsty's Dad took her to a jumble sale in the school hall.

Dad was looking for old postcards. He said Kirsty could have an ice-cream if she found a postcard from Russia.

Kirsty found a postcard showing a camel.
"Is this alright?" she asked.
"No, that's Egypt. Keep looking." Dad replied.

Read everything as carefully as you can.

Where was the jumble sale?

....

Kirsty found a postcard showing lots of skyscrapers.
"Is this alright?" she asked.
"No, that's the United States, but keep looking." Dad replied.

Kirsty was getting bored. She wanted the ice-cream though.

Just then she spotted a postcard showing a village covered in snow.
"I think this is Russia," Kirsty said.
"That's exactly what I wanted," cried Dad.

Where was the postcard with the skyscrapers from?

....

What was covered in snow?

....

Don't be a mug and miss things out...
Read every single word on the page.

Section Two — Reading Comprehension

Answering the Questions

To answer any question you have to look at the bit of writing.

What should you do **when the eggs are cool**?

The words from the question can help you find the answer.

- When the eggs are cool peel them and slice them.
- Spread some butter on the bread.

Now you can answer the question.

What should you do when the eggs are cool?

You should peel them and slice them.

Q1 Read this piece of writing and **answer** the question.

Mustard and Cress

Mustard and cress are small green plants.

A lot of people like to cut them up and eat them in sandwiches. Cress tastes like lettuce. Mustard has a hot peppery flavour.

What does cress taste like?

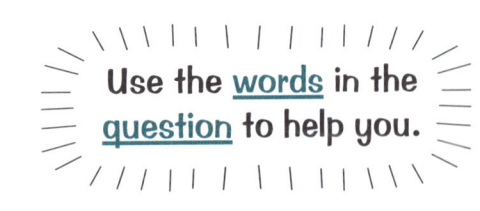

....

Use the words in the question to help you.

Get your answer from the bit of writing.

Section Two — Reading Comprehension

Q2 Now read these **instructions**, and **answer** the questions.

Cress is easy to grow indoors.

- Place 4 pieces of kitchen towel on a plate and pour on a glass of water.
- Sprinkle cress seeds thinly on the paper.
- Put the plate in a sunny place.
- Remember to KEEP THE PAPER WET.
- After 3 days the cress will be ready to eat.
- Cut it with scissors and sprinkle on sandwiches or salads.

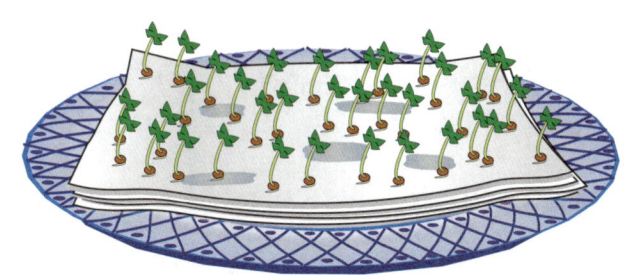

1   How many pieces of kitchen towel should you use?

   ....

2   What would be the best place to put the plate?

   ☐ in a cupboard   ☐ by a window

   ☐ next to some scissors ☐ in your bedroom

3   Why do you think KEEP THE PAPER WET is written in capital letters?

   ☐ because of the paper   ☐ because it is angry

   ☐ to show it is important   ☐ so it is easier

Don't go making things up...
The answer's *in the writing*.

Section Two — Reading Comprehension

Answering the Questions

Sometimes you have to <u>read extra carefully</u> to find the answers.
Read the <u>beginning</u> of this story.

Sandcastles

Sarah was building a sandcastle.
"I want a go," said Pete. But Sarah was enjoying herself too much.
"No!" she said.

1   What did Pete want to do?

[✓] help build the sandcastle   [ ] make sandwiches

[ ] go for a swim   [ ] go home

Sarah was <u>building a sandcastle</u>. Pete wanted a go <u>too</u>.
So <u>this</u> is the right answer.

**Look carefully at the story.
<u>All</u> the answers are there.**

Q: **Read the rest of this story and answer the questions.**

"Don't worry," said Mum. "Here's another bucket.
Now you can both build a castle."

Sarah and Pete worked all afternoon. Soon their castles
had walls and turrets and moats.

2   Write down **2** other things that Pete and Sarah's castles had.

a) *walls*

b) ....

c) ....

Section Two — Reading Comprehension

At last they finished.
Pete looked at Sarah's castle, and Sarah looked at Peter's.

"Mine's the best!" said Pete.
"No, mine's the best," Sarah replied.

While Sarah and Pete were arguing, the sea was splashing quickly towards their castles. It came rushing through the moats, bursting through the walls and knocking down the towers.

"My castle!" wailed Sarah and Pete together.
But both castles were gone, and the water rushed all the way up to their feet.

Useful Word
wailed - said sadly

"I don't care! I'll build another castle tomorrow!" said Pete.
"Or we could build a really strong one together," said Sarah.
"One that can stand up to the sea?" asked Pete. "Brilliant."

"If you do it together, who knows?" said Mum happily.

---

3   Did Sarah agree with Pete that his sandcastle was best?

   ....

4   How do you think Sarah and Pete felt when they saw the sea wash the sandcastles away?

   ☐ sick   ☐ sad

   ☐ angry   ☐ cheerful

5   Why didn't Pete care that his sandcastle was gone?

   ....

Sniff out the answers...
You've got to look for them in the story.

Section Two — Reading Comprehension

Answering the Questions

For some questions you have to look at the whole piece of writing to find the answer.

Choose another good title for the poem.

☐ Sun and Rain   ☐ Lively Lobsters

☐ A Picnic Shark   ☐ I'm Not Scared

You can't answer this question now. Read the whole poem first.

Q: Read this poem. Then answer the questions.

Beside the Seaside

Sun heating,
Waves beating,
Sea splashing,
Waves crashing.

    Gulls floating,
    People boating,
    Air bracing,
    Boats racing.

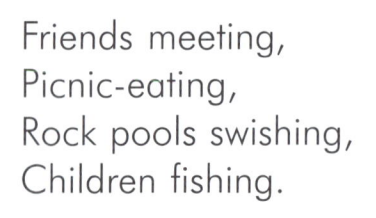

Friends meeting,
Picnic-eating,
Rock pools swishing,
Children fishing.

    People swimming,
    Sun dimming,
    Rain lashing,
    Lightning flashing.

Storm blowing,
People going.

Section Two — Reading Comprehension

Sometimes you have to read all the writing to find the right answer.

1. What is this poem about?

    ☐ what happens in one day at the seaside
    ☐ a school trip
    ☐ how to sail a boat
    ☐ my holidays last year

2. **Floating** rhymes with **boating**.
   Find two more words that rhyme with each other.

   ....

3. The word **splashing** sounds like water moving.
   Find two more words that sound like water moving.

   ....

4. At the end it says **People going**. Why do you think they are going?

   ....

Glue your eyeballs to the page...
For some questions you have to read it all again.

Section Two — Reading Comprehension

Saying What You Think

One special kind of question asks what you think about the bits of writing.

Why do you think it is a good thing to learn to swim?

Why do you think Harry was so happy when he got home?

The reason in your answer has to be something from the writing. If you just put down any old thing you could get it completely wrong.

Don't make your reasons up. Get them from the writing.

Q1   Read the information on this page and the next. Then answer the questions.

SHARK FACTS

- Sharks are a type of fish. There are about 340 different kinds of shark.
- Sharks are fast swimmers. Blue sharks can swim at forty miles an hour.
- Sharks have an excellent sense of smell.
- Sharks have hundreds of sharp teeth.
- Sharks sometimes attack people, but it doesn't happen often.
- Some kinds of shark may die out because fishermen have caught too many.

Dwarf sharks are the smallest sharks. They are less than 30cm long.

You don't see that everyday.

The biggest shark is the whale shark. Whale sharks can be 15 metres long.

1   What is the smallest type of shark called?

....

Section Two — Reading Comprehension

SHARKS — AWFUL OR AWESOME?

> Sharks are nasty, dangerous creatures.
> I can't go surfing when there are sharks around.
> I don't mind if I never see another shark as long as I live.

George
Champion surfer

> There is no other animal like the shark.
> If we don't protect sharks from fishermen they will die out.
> They aren't as dangerous as people think.

Miranda
Shark scientist

2 Who doesn't like sharks?

   ....

3 Miranda thinks we should protect sharks because

   ☐ they are nasty.   ☐ there is no other animal like the shark.

   ☐ we could eat them.   ☐ they swim very fast.

4 Look back at all the information about sharks. Do **you** think we should protect sharks?

   You have to look back at the writing.

   ☐ Yes   ☐ No

   Why?..

   ....

Strain your brain...
Find the answer in the writing.

Section Two — Reading Comprehension

Practice Reading Comprehension

Here's a <u>last bit</u> of reading for you — <u>dive in</u>. Do the reading, <u>then</u> the questions.

Submarines

Submarines are special boats that can go underwater. They can dive much deeper than people can. As you dive deeper, the water pressure gets stronger. Submarines are made of very thick steel so the water pressure can't crush them.

Inside a submarine there are special containers called ballast tanks. If these are full of air, the submarine floats. If they are full of water, the submarine dives. The sailors can pump water or air into the ballast tanks to make the submarine go up or down.

Every submarine has an air supply so that the people on board can breathe, even though they are underwater. Some submarines can stay under the surface of the sea for months at a time.

1\. What kind of boat is a submarine?

   ....

2\. If the ballast tanks are full of air what does the submarine do?

   ☐ go forwards   ☐ pump water

   ☐ dive   ☐ float

   Remember to look <u>in the writing</u> for your answer.

3\. What allows the people in submarines to breathe underwater?

   ....

Section Two — Reading Comprehension

Periscopes

When a submarine is under the sea, the captain uses a periscope to see things on the surface. A periscope is a tube or a box with a mirror at each end.

How a Periscope Works

You can use a periscope to see things that are higher than you or round a corner.

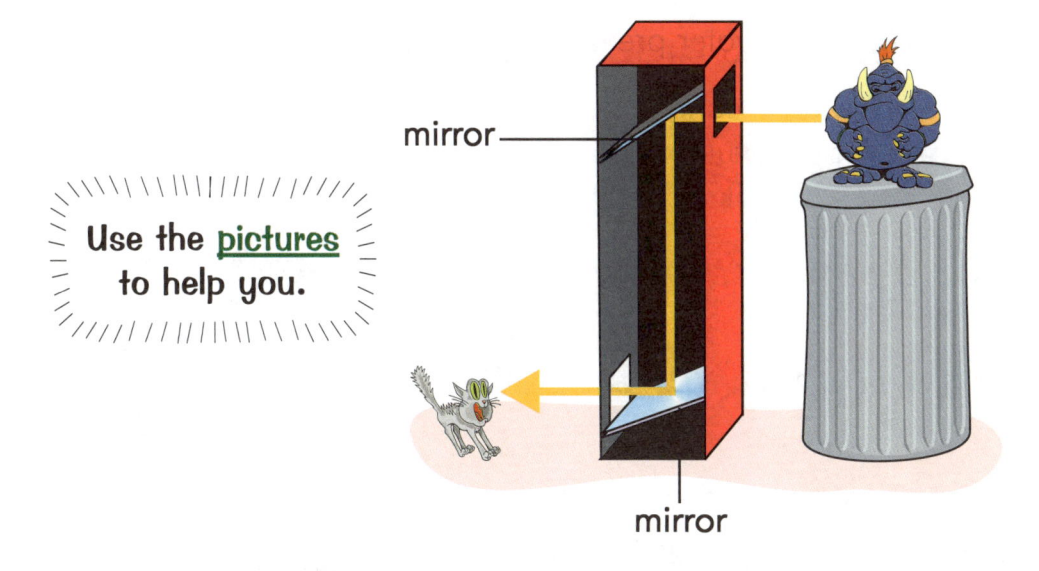

Use the pictures to help you.

- A picture of the monster reflects in the top mirror.
- Then it reflects in the bottom mirror.
- The cat sees the monster in the bottom mirror.

---

4   How many mirrors do you need to make a periscope?

    ....

Don't make any answers up.

5   a)   What does the captain of a submarine use a periscope for?

    ☐ to see the other people in the submarine   ☐ to catch sharks

    ☐ to see things on the surface   ☐ to float

    b)   What **2** things can you use a periscope for?

    ....

Section Two — Reading Comprehension

Starting and Ending Sentences

Every sentence must begin with a **capital letter** and end with a **full stop**.

A sentence looks like this**.**

Q1 Underline the **capital letters** and circle the **full stops**.

My mum's really scared of spiders.

My brother's got a pet tarantula.

Eric dances with a top hat and a stick.

Q2 **Start** each sentence with the word in the box.

Don't forget the capital letter at the beginning.

| the | *The* .... trees are very old. |

| it | .... was bright. |

| my | .... brother's spider is scared of centipedes. |

| lots | .... of people are scared of spiders. |

| some | .... spiders eat birds. |

Section Three — Writing Skills

Always use capital letters and full stops in every sentence.

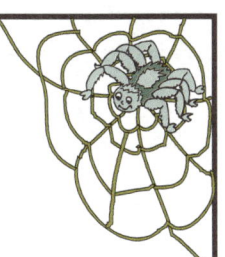

Q3 Use **all** the words in each box to write a **proper sentence**.

Don't forget the capital letters.

it, dark, very, was — It was very dark.

his, broke, Roger, leg — ....

the, scary, was, robot — ....

hates, Randolph, carrots — ....

in, it, the, fell, pond — ....

I sentence you to learn this...
Start with a capital and finish with a full stop.

Section Three — Writing Skills

Questions and Exclamations

Questions end with a special full stop. It's called a question mark.

What's going on?

You use a question mark if someone asks a question.

Q1 Put a **tick** next to the **questions** in this table.

	Is this a question?
✓	Do you like this song?
	No, not really.
	I think it's great.
	Do you really?

A question always ends in a question mark.

Q2 Look at each of these sentences.
If it's a question, put a **question mark** at the end.

If it's not a question, put a full stop.

Which ingredient makes cakes rise **?**

It is the egg **.**

Are you sure

Yes I am

How do you know

Section Three — Writing Skills

Some sentences end with an exclamation mark.

That can't be right!

You use them to show surprises, shouting or strong feelings.

Q3 Underline **four exclamations** in this bit of writing.

"Hello there!" said Bill.
"Hi!" said Sally. "Come with me."
"What are we going to see?" asked Bill.
"A dragon!" exclaimed Sally.
"Gosh!" said Bill. "Is it real?"

Write **two more** exclamations of your own here:

....

....

Q4 **Fill in** the gaps with a **question mark** or an **exclamation mark**.

That's amazing !.....

What is it .....

There's an ant playing the violin .....

What's he playing .....

Happy Birthday .....

Time to make your mark...
Questions and exclamations — get practising now.

Section Three — Writing Skills

Don't Use 'and' Too Much

Lots of people use **and** all the time in their writing.
Don't do it — it's really boring.

Try using some different words instead.

Ellen danced, **but** Mary bounced.

Ellen danced **when** Mary bounced.

Ellen danced, **so** Mary bounced.

These words are MUCH MORE INTERESTING than 'and'.

> Don't use AND all the time.
> Try some different words instead.

Q1 Underline the word which **makes the most sense** in each sentence.

The actor finished the play (**then** / while) took a bow.

Geoffrey locked his door (but / so) he felt safe.

We played eye-spy (while / and) the train went by.

Pick it up (and / then) pass it on.

Katy is tall (so / but) Suzanne is taller.

Larry plays golf (while / so) Sarah plays chess.

Section Three — Writing Skills

Q2 **Fill the gap** in each sentence with the **right word** from the cloud.

Cloud words: but, but, when, so

Find the word that fits best in each sentence.

The shops are still open .... we can get Paula a present.

Rajesh remembered his coat .... he left his hat behind.

We were playing a game .... you came in.

I like bananas .... I'm not a monkey.

Q3 Write these sentences out again with a **new linking word**.

I had a cola and I didn't have any ice.

....

I didn't win the match and I'm going swimming.

....

....

Oi! Keep your 'and's off...

Don't use 'and' too much. Try 'but', 'so' or 'then'.

Section Three — Writing Skills

Use Interesting Words

Make your sentences more interesting by using different words like these:

John was scared **although** the light was on.

The pirates gulped **because** the crocodile was huge.

These sorts of words join the different parts of the sentence to each other.

Q1 Draw a line under the **joining words** in each sentence.

Chris was scared <u>because</u> he'd heard a strange noise.

It was dark because the power had gone off.

The mermaid sang although she was tired.

Q2 Choose the word that **fits best** in each sentence.

although
because

I love seafood ...*although*... I don't eat it often.

John ran off .... he was scared.

Brian was shocked .... he saw a ghost in a bubble.

.... it won't be pleasant, someone must go.

These words make your writing **more interesting**.

Section Three — Writing Skills

Here are some great words to use. They tell you <u>when</u> something's happened:

<u>When</u> you get there, you must ring me.

Turn the handle <u>as</u> you push the button.

Q3 **Finish** each sentence with the **right word** from the list.

While you're here, could you fix the door?

Wipe your feet .... you come in.

Shelley screamed .... the door blew open.

.... dinner you must brush your teeth.

when, before, after, while

Q4 Write **three sentences** using the joining words on the plank.

then   so   before

Any of these words is better than 'and'.

① The ship hit a big rock .... it sank.

Write two more sentences here:

② ....

③ ....

Use interesting words...
You'll get loads more marks.

Section Three — Writing Skills

Write In Clear Sentences

If you keep your sentences <u>short</u>, they're <u>easier</u> to read.

The clown went to bed. ✓

<u>Don't</u> keep on adding new bits. It's silly, and it's <u>boring</u>.

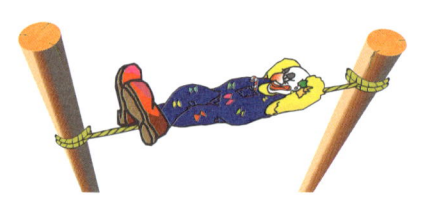

The clown put on his pyjamas and brushed his teeth and went to bed and read a book. ✗

There are <u>too many</u> 'ands'.

If a sentence has <u>more than one</u> 'and', it's <u>too long</u>.

Q1 Put a **cross** beside each sentence that's **too long**.

We went to the park and we had a battle and Josh won and he was King.

We watched the Chinese acrobats and we were amazed.

The circus came to town and there were clowns and they were very funny.

It's the <u>same</u> with '<u>then</u>'. More than one 'then' is <u>too many</u>.

Then we went to the fair, then we ate candy floss, then we went home. ✗

Q2 Put a big **cross** beside the sentences with too many '**then**'s. Put a **tick** beside the sentences that are **alright**.

The acrobats jumped on trampolines then they did backflips.

A man was juggling four balls then he juggled five then he juggled some fish.

Next we saw a tightrope walker, then the clowns came back.

Section Three — Writing Skills

Two short sentences are better than one huge messy one.

Q3 **Rewrite** these long sentences as **two short sentences**.

Miss Tina is the tightrope walker and she never falls off.

Miss Tina is the tightrope walker.

She never falls off.

The magician could make rabbits appear because he was very clever.

....

....

The clown grabbed the balloon then he floated up towards the sky.

....

....

Keep your sentences short...
Don't try and cram too much in.

Section Three — Writing Skills

Speech Marks

Speech marks are little squiggles that show the words someone actually said.

"They're big cats!" said Robbie.

Q1 Circle the speech marks in each sentence.

"Where are we going on holiday?" asked Jen.

"We're going to the jungle." answered Sam.

"There are animals," said Sam. "Lots of them."

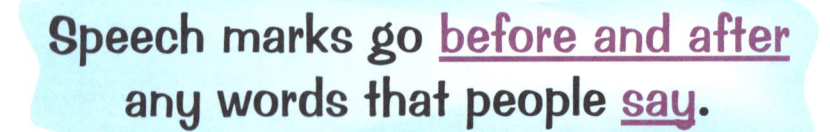

Speech marks go before and after any words that people say.

We go before the speech. We go after it.

Q2 Fill in any missing speech marks.

Graham said, "I don't feel very well."

"Have you got a fever?" asked the doctor.

No," replied Graham, "but I have a pet tiger.

And where is it now? wondered Dr Jones.

Section Three — Writing Skills

Q3 Fill in these sentences to show what each person is **saying**.

Michael gasped, "What's that?"

Don't forget the **speech marks**.

.... called Freddy.

.... Cheetah whimpered.

.... chuckled Lucy.

Pssst — a word in your ear...
Speech marks go round what's actually said.

Section Three — Writing Skills

Planning a Story

It's easier to write stories if you **plan** them before you start. Think of...

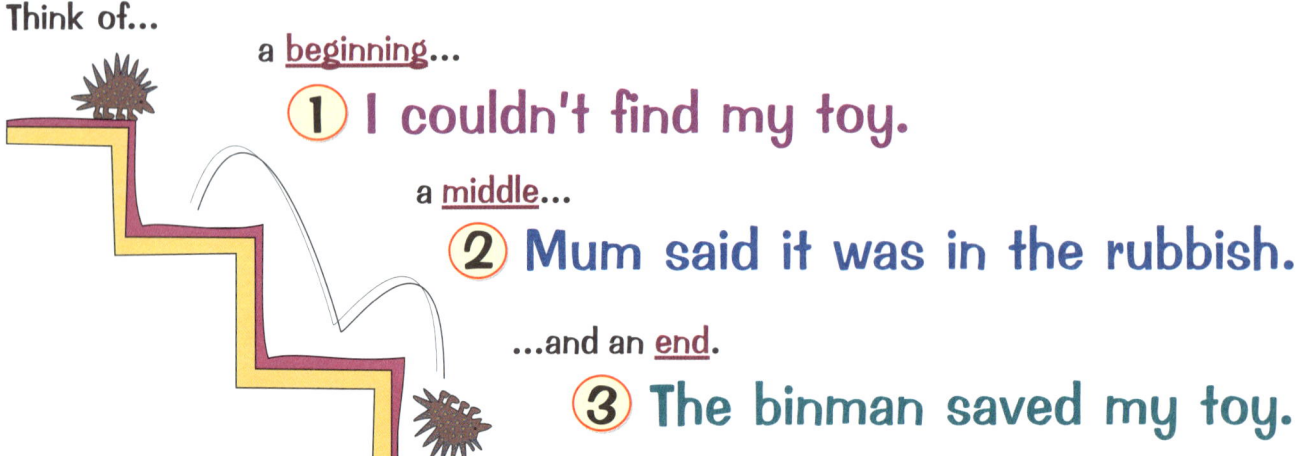

a <u>beginning</u>...
① I couldn't find my toy.

a <u>middle</u>...
② Mum said it was in the rubbish.

...and an <u>end</u>.
③ The binman saved my toy.

Q1 Follow the **lines** to read the **story plan**.

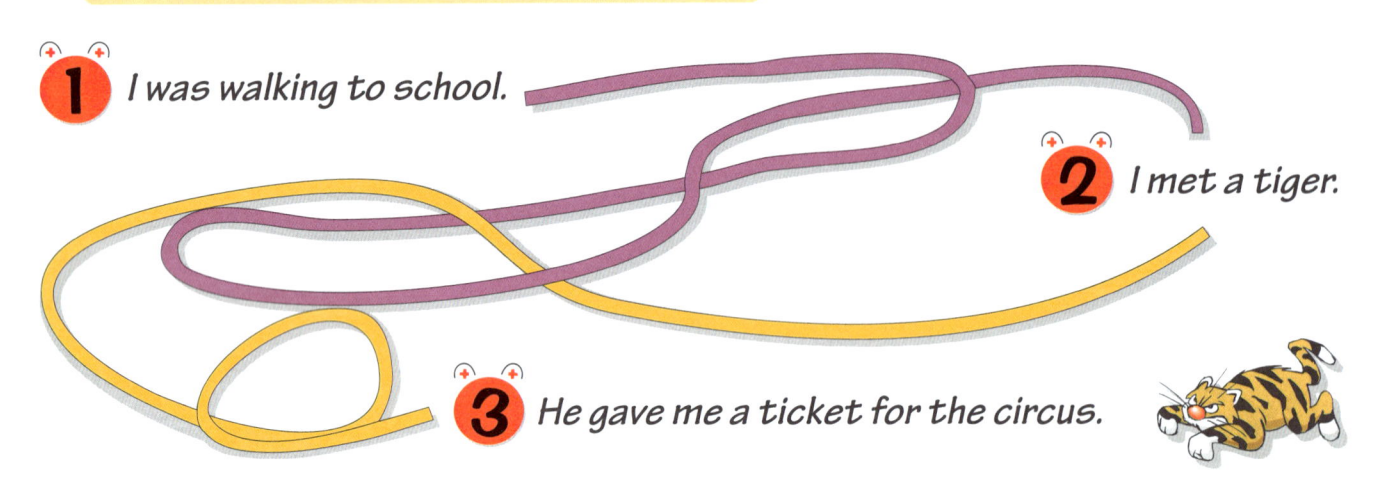

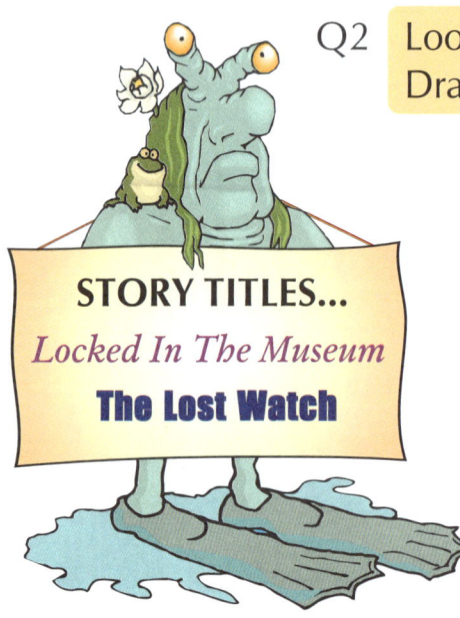

① I was walking to school.

② I met a tiger.

③ He gave me a ticket for the circus.

Q2 Look at the two **story titles**. Draw a line to match each one to the right **story plan**.

1 I was at the seaside.
2 A fisherman lost his watch. Later I found it.
3 The fisherman gave me lots of fish.

1 I went to a museum. I was locked in.
2 I had to stay all night. I slept in Queen Victoria's bed.
3 Her ghost read me a story.

STORY TITLES...
Locked In The Museum
The Lost Watch

Section Four — Writing Stories

Think of a beginning, a middle and an end before you start writing.

Q3 These **plans** have got bits missing. Fill in the gaps.

This plan needs a beginning.

① *We ran out of bread.*
   I decided to make some.

② I went to watch TV while the bread was baking.

③ I fell asleep, and the bread burnt.

This plan needs a middle.

① Gita's mum was out.

② ....
   ....

③ Gita hid all the pieces under the sofa.

This plan needs an end.

① It rained all night.

② In the morning, downstairs was full of water. We couldn't get out of the house.

③ ....
   ....

Write better stories...
Think about the **beginning**, the **middle**, and the **end**.

Section Four — Writing Stories

Starting a Story

When you start a story, say what's going on right at the start.
Here are three ways of starting a story.

You can say who it's about.
Carla is an explorer.

You can say where it happened.
Grandma's farm was by the lake.

You can say when it happened.
Spring came late last year.

Q1 These stories **start** in different ways.
Answer the **question** about each one.

Uncle Walter was sick of the bears eating his food.
He decided to play a trick on them.

Who is this story about?

Uncle Walter

It was a normal, boring Sunday until the volcano erupted.

When did this story happen?

....

Last winter there was a huge snow storm.
The school in Mooseville was closed for a week.

Where did this story happen?

....

Section Four — Writing Stories

Q2   Does the story start by telling you **who**, **where** or **when**? Tick the box.

Mr Motley wears red and yellow every day.
The other park rangers wear green shirts and trousers.

who ✓   where ☐   when ☐

Right in the middle of town there was a cake shop.
It was called Custards. That's where I found the mouse.

who ☐   where ☐   when ☐

To start a story off say **who** it's about,
where it happened, or **when** it happened.

Q3   Use the pictures to help you **start** writing this story.

You don't have to write the whole thing — just the start.

The Sneakiest Salmon

....

....

....

Give your story a good start...
Write about a person, a place or a time.

Section Four — Writing Stories

Using Describing Words

Describing words tell you what things are like.

This is a describing word.

The massive whale swam slowly.

This is a describing word, too.

Q1 Underline the describing words in these sentences.

I found an <u>old</u> map.
The paper was <u>crumbly</u>. I held it <u>carefully</u>.
I could see a little island on the map.

I went on a long journey to find the island.
I walked slowly over hot, dry deserts.

I crossed high, snowy mountains.
I sailed endlessly over rough seas.

At last I arrived at the beautiful island.
I decided to stay for a long time.

Q2 You can use **colours** to describe things.
What colour are these things?

a *brown* coconut   a .... apple   a .... avocado   a .... plum

Say how the things in your story look.

Section Four — Writing Stories

Q3 How do the people in these pictures **feel**?
Choose the **best** describing word.

(hungry)   cold   bored   scared
itchy   sleepy   happy   cross

Say how things in your story make people feel.

Q4 Choose the **best** describing word to fill the gap in each sentence.

~~long~~   black   loudly
~~little~~   lonely   ~~curved~~   white

A _little_ toucan sat on my window sill.

It had a _long_ _curved_ beak.

Its feathers were .... and ....

The toucan tapped .... on the window.

It looked very ....

Use describing words in your stories...
Stories with no describing words are boring.

Section Four — Writing Stories

Using Different Words

People use these words <u>all the time</u>. They're <u>really boring</u>.

got   said   went

Try and use <u>different words</u> instead.

picked up   shouted   ran

<u>They</u> make stories <u>more exciting</u>.

Q1 You can use all the words in the list instead of **went**. Find them in the puzzle.

~~rushed~~

walked

ran

flew

left

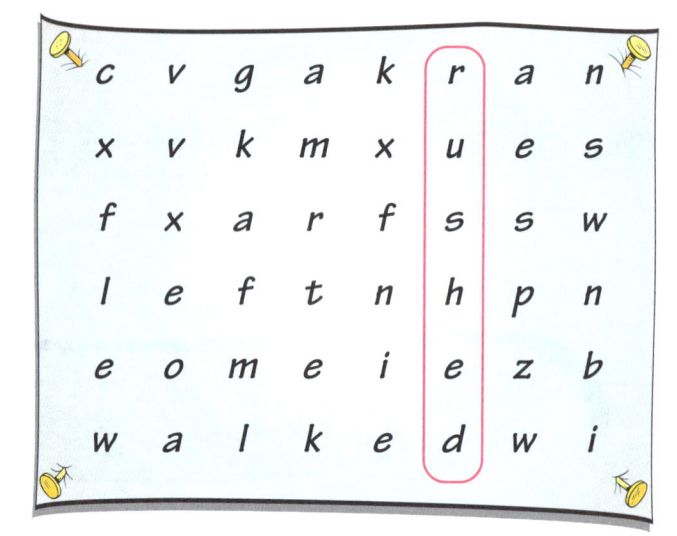

c	v	g	a	k	r	a	n
x	v	k	m	x	u	e	s
f	x	a	r	f	s	s	w
l	e	f	t	n	h	p	n
e	o	m	e	i	e	z	b
w	a	l	k	e	d	w	i

"I just want to play with you!"

Q2 Choose the best word to use instead of **got** or **get**.

My brother *got* measles.

(caught)   bought

Mum and I *got* the number 36 bus.

took   washed

Mum *got* some medicine for my brother from the chemist.

squashed   picked up

Section Four — Writing Stories

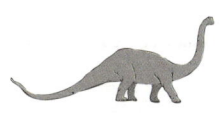

Steer clear of got, said and went.

Q3 **Fill in the gaps** with words from the dinosaur egg.

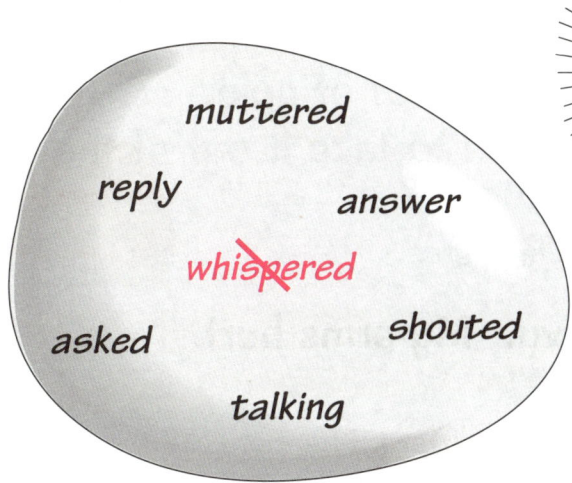

These are all good words to use instead of said.

Egg words: muttered, reply, answer, ~~whispered~~, asked, shouted, talking

"Where's the dinosaur room, please?" I ....whispered.....

The guard didn't ....

I tried .... a little bit louder.

SILENCE IN THE MUSEUM

"Excuse me," I ...., "Where's the dinosaur room?"

He still didn't ....

I thought maybe he was deaf, so this time
I ...., "Where are the dinosaurs?"

The guard looked angry.
"Can't you read the sign?" he ....

Better not be boring...
Use the most exciting words you possibly can.

Section Four — Writing Stories

Ending a Story

Good stories have good endings.
The end of a story has to be different to the middle.

① I was walking in the forest.

② I found a pot of gold.
I started to take it out of the forest.

This is a bad ending. Nothing different happens.

③ The gold was heavy. My arms hurt.

This is good because something completely different happens.

③ At the edge of the forest the gold turned to water.

Q1 Tick the better ending for the story.

① We were going home from school.

② The bus didn't come.
It started to snow.
I was very cold.

③ Two hours later it was still snowing.
I was still cold. ☐

③ At last the bus came.
The driver gave us all hot chocolate. ☐

**Make the ending different to the middle.
That way everyone knows the story's over.**

Section Four — Writing Stories

Q2 **Write endings for these stories. Use the pictures to help you.**

① My grandma lives in a cottage in the woods.
I went to stay with her.

② In the night I heard horrible, scary noises.
I thought it was ghosts.

③ ....

....

① Colin was looking for nuts.
He needed enough to last all winter.

② There were no nuts on the hazelnut tree.
There were no nuts on the walnut tree.

③ ....

....

① Louise lost her dog in the woods.

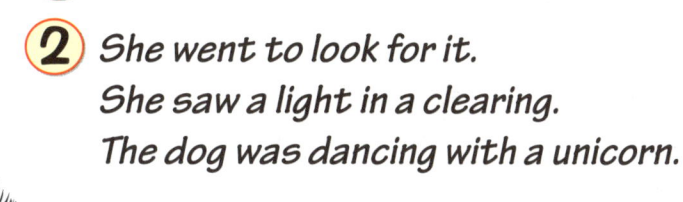

② She went to look for it.
She saw a light in a clearing.
The dog was dancing with a unicorn.

③ ....

....

Do a fantastic finish...
Make it really obvious **it's the end.**

Section Four — Writing Stories

You Write a Story

It's your turn to write a story, so make it a good 'un.

Q1 Look at the **title** and the **pictures**. Then write a **quick plan**.

The Whale and The Owl and the Pussycat — PLAN

① ....

....

② ....

....

....

③ ....

....

Q2 Now you're ready to **write** the story.

The Whale and The Owl and the Pussycat

Put the start of the story here.

Describe what things look like and feel like.

My tooth hurts!

....

....

....

....

Section Four — Writing Stories

Write the middle of the story here.

....
....
....
....
....
....

Try not to use the boring words — got, went and said.

The end goes here. Make it different.

....
....
....

That's all folks...
Don't forget to make a plan. And always end it well.

Section Four — Writing Stories

Titles and Introductions

It's really important to start any bit of writing well.
You need a title and an introduction.

The title should say what the writing is about.

Machines at home

This article tells you how things at home like toasters and vacuum cleaners work.

Toasters work by making the bread very hot so that it goes brown and turns into toast. When the toast is ready, the toaster switches off and the toast pops up out of the toaster.

The introduction tells you more about the writing.

Don't make your title longer than one line.

Use big writing to make the title clear. You could draw a line under it too.

Looking After Pets

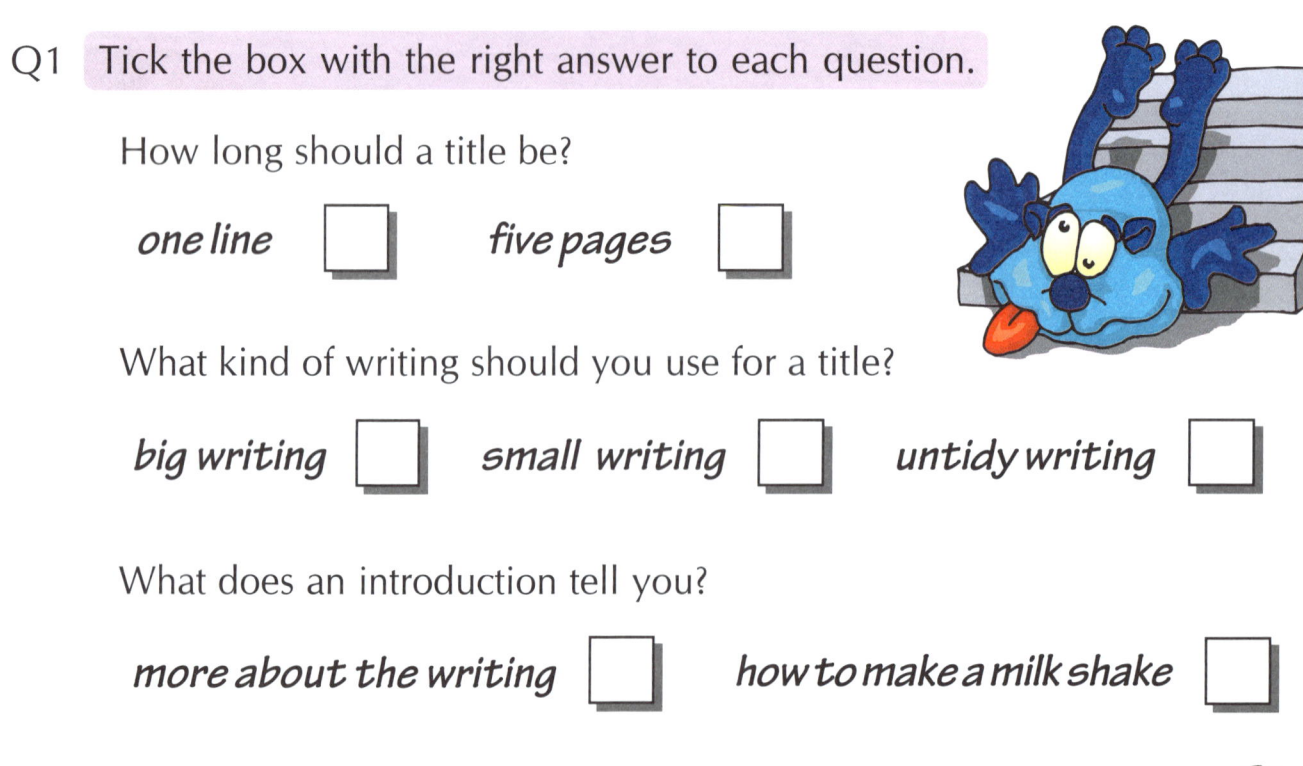

Q1 Tick the box with the right answer to each question.

How long should a title be?

one line ☐   five pages ☐

What kind of writing should you use for a title?

big writing ☐   small writing ☐   untidy writing ☐

What does an introduction tell you?

more about the writing ☐   how to make a milk shake ☐

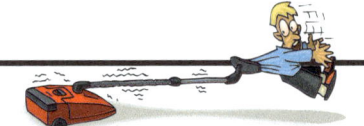

Section Five — Other Writing

Q2 Read each of these bits of writing. Then **write in** a **title** for each one.

REMEMBER: the title tells you what the writing is about.

1
....
We need to eat plenty of fruit and vegetables to keep us healthy. If you eat too many sweets, you get holes in your teeth.

2
....
• Woodlice live under stones. They are grey and hard on the outside. They've got lots of legs and two big feelers.
• Ladybirds live on plants. They are red with black spots. They eat greenfly, which is good for gardens, because greenfly are a pest.
• Centipedes have a hundred legs. They are usually shiny brown. Centipedes live under stones, like woodlice.

3
....
Torquay is in South Devon. It's a popular place for seaside holidays. It has three sandy beaches, and there's a harbour where you can go on fishing trips.

Q3 Write an **introduction** for the **second bit** of writing in question 2.

....
....
....

Introductions are ace...
They tell everyone <u>what you're writing about</u>.

Section Five — Other Writing

Sub-headings

Sub-headings are cool. They're like mini titles to break up long bits of writing. You should use them in your information writing.

This is a sub-heading.

Ferrets

This is the main title.

Ferrets are popular but unusual pets.

General Information
A male ferret is called a hob and a female ferret is called a jill. Baby ferrets are called kits. A ferret can live for 6-10 years.

Ferret Behaviour
Ferrets love to play. When they are excited, they race around and dance. They enjoy hiding small objects like toys, keys and TV remote controls, so these things should be kept out of their way.

More sub-headings.

Ferrets like to dance.

Looking After a Ferret
Ferrets are friendly, but they need to be handled with care. They aren't suitable for very young children because they can bite when they get frightened. As long as they feel safe, they'll be fine.

This bit of writing about ferrets is broken up into three sections. Each section has a new sub-heading.

Q1 Write down **all three sub-headings** from the bit of writing about ferrets.

....

....

....

Section Five — Other Writing

Q2 Look at these two sections from a **report** about hamsters. Write a **sub-heading** to go with **each section**.

....

In the wild, hamsters live in burrows. They sleep during the day and come out only at night.

....

Hamsters are easy pets to look after. You can buy hamster food from a pet shop. They also like apples, celery and carrot. It's a good idea to give them a piece of wood to chew on, too.

Sub-headings make your writing clear. Use them for reports or information writing.

Q3 Imagine you're writing a **booklet** about **animals**. Think of **three sub-headings** for the booklet.

① ....

② ....

③ ....

Don't be a scaredy-mouse...

Put sub-headings in your writing to make it clear.

Section Five — Other Writing

Bullet Points

These big <u>dots</u> are called <u>bullet points</u>.

- They're <u>great</u>.
- They make <u>information</u> easy to read.
- They'll make you look dead <u>clever</u>.

When you write a <u>new fact</u>, stick a <u>bullet point</u> in front of it.

Q1 **Draw a circle** around **all** the bullet points in this piece of writing.

Bone Facts

Everybody has bones, but most of us don't know anything about them. Here are some bone facts.

- Bones are hard. They protect our soft insides.
- Bones work like levers to help us move and lift things.
- We need to drink milk and eat vegetables to keep our bones strong.

Q2 There are **four facts** about our bodies in the list below. Three bullet points are **missing**. Put them in the right places.

- The heart is the organ that pumps blood around the body.

  The stomach breaks down food so we can digest it.

  Eyes are for seeing.

  Ears are used for hearing.

Don't forget: each <u>new bit</u> needs a <u>new</u> bullet point.

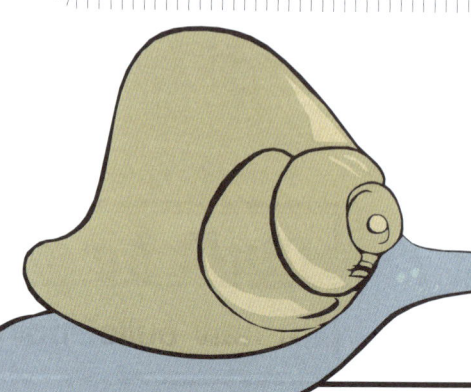

Section Five — Other Writing

Q3 Find **two facts** and write them out as **two new bullet points**.

The Truth about Teeth
Teeth are hard bone-like things in our mouths. Sugar attacks your teeth causing decay. If you want to take care of your teeth, don't eat sugary foods like sweets, and brush your teeth twice a day.

- *Teeth are bone-like things in your mouth.*
- ....
  ....
- ....
  ....

Q4 Write out **two facts** from this box using **bullet points** for **each new fact**.

We need teeth to chew our food. Different kinds of teeth do different jobs. Incisors cut food, canines tear food, and molars chew food.
The first set of teeth a person has are called milk teeth. As you get older they are pushed out by the adult teeth.

Put your writing in here.

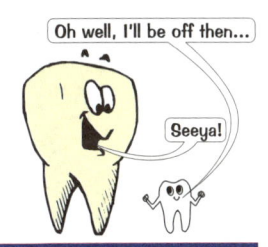

Bullet points drive me dotty...
A new bullet point for <u>each new fact</u> — lovely.

Section Five — Other Writing

Looking for Facts

When you write a booklet or a report, you need to look for facts to put in it.

1) Look at the books you've read together in class.
2) Think about the main facts.
3) Use the facts to write your booklet.

Here are some short bits from a book about a man called George Stephenson.

Q1 Answer the questions about the main facts in this bit.

> George Stephenson was born in 1781. His family was poor, so he went to work instead of going to school. He learnt to read at evening classes.
> When he was twenty-one, he got a job repairing engines in a coal mine. He took them apart and found out how they worked.

Who is it about? ......George Stephenson......

When was he born? ....

Where did he learn to read?

....

Where did he repair engines? ....

Q2 **Underline** the **main facts** in this bit of the book. The first two are done for you.

> In <u>1814</u> Stephenson built his <u>first steam locomotive</u>. It could pull thirty tons of coal up a hill at 4 mph. Over the next five years he built sixteen more engines.

Section Five — Other Writing

Q3 Write down **two facts** from this bit of the book.

> In those days, horses were used to pull carts along railways. George Stephenson's railway was the first one that used engines instead of horses. Stephenson said that one of his steam engines could do the work of fifty horses.

Well, isn't that something!

....

....

Find the facts before you start writing.

Q4 Write **two sentences** with facts about the Stockton-Darlington railway.

> In 1821, George Stephenson was put in charge of building a railway from Stockton to Darlington. Work on the railway track began in 1822.
>
> The line was officially opened on 27th September, 1825. The first trains were very slow — it took 2 hours to go 9 miles!

① ....

....

② ....

....

Find the facts — at a factory...
Use short, clear sentences.

Section Five — Other Writing

Endings

Endings are dead important. You don't just need them for stories. Look at the ending of this bit of a booklet about phones.

Phones in the Past

Telephones were invented in the 1870s, but it took a long time before most houses had them. The first telephones had no buttons or dial.

Nowadays phones are much easier to use. I'm glad I don't have to use an old phone.

This is a good ending.

A good ending says what you think.

You need to put a good ending on every bit of information writing you do.

Q1 Tick the boxes with the **right answers** to these questions.

Are endings important?

☐ Yes   ☐ No

What does a good ending say?

☐ goodbye   ☐ what you think

Which **three** kinds of writing need a good ending?

☐ handwriting   ☐ music   ☐ information writing

☐ letters   ☐ stories   ☐ French

Section Five — Other Writing

Here are the endings to three different bits of information writing. Read them carefully, and look at the list of titles next to them.

Q2 **Match** each ending to the **correct** title.

Endings

Elephants are beautiful animals, and I think they shouldn't be allowed to die out.

People's homes were different then. I'm glad I don't live in a Victorian house!

If you like a good story then you should read this book.

Titles

Frog Is a Hero — a Book Review

Discovering Elephants

Inside a Victorian House

Q3 Read this bit of writing about Florence Nightingale and write a **good ending** for it.

Florence Nightingale was born in 1820. She was born in Italy, but her parents were English.

In 1848, she decided to be a nurse. In 1854, there was a war in the Crimea. Florence went there to care for the soldiers.

She made sure that hospitals were clean and sick people were looked after properly. The soldiers loved her. Nowadays she is remembered as one of the founders of modern nursing.

....

....

Your ending could say why we should be grateful to Florence.

It's the end of the line...
A good ending says what you think.

Section Five — Other Writing

Practice Writing Exercise

Here's a **full-length** practice exercise. Read through **all** the bits of writing first.

Elephants in the Wild

There are two kinds of elephant — the African elephant and the Indian elephant.

African Elephants	Indian Elephants
Bigger ears Small, flat head	Smaller ears Big, domed head

An African Elephant

The Trunk

Elephants use their trunk to pick leaves off trees to eat. They drink by sucking water up through their trunk and squirting it into their mouths. They wash by squirting water over themselves through their trunks.

Elephants in Danger

Elephants are in great danger of becoming extinct. African elephants are killed for their tusks, which are made into ivory. Wildlife reserves have been set up to protect the elephants.

It is illegal to hunt elephants inside reserves. We can help elephants by making sure we never buy anything made from ivory.

Elephant facts and figures
- The African elephant is the largest living land animal, weighing up to 8 tons and standing 3 to 4m tall.
- The Indian elephant weighs 5 tons, and is 3m tall.
- Elephants live to 60 or 70 years old.
- Elephants can eat over 225kg of grass and leaves a day.

Section Five — Other Writing

Q: Q: Use the information on the last page to help you write a **short report** about elephants.

Think about how to <u>start</u> your writing.

Think about how to make it <u>interesting</u>.

Think about how to <u>end</u> it.

Write your report in this space.

Put your <u>title</u> here

Use <u>sub-headings</u> and <u>bullet points</u> too.

<u>Be an elephant — never forget...</u>
It's time to <u>practise</u> what you've learnt.

Section Five — Other Writing

Answers

Pages 38-39 Using Different Words

Q1

```
c v g a k (r a n)
x v k m x (u) e s
f x a r f (s) s w
(l e f t) n (h) p n
e o m e i (e) z b
(w a l k e d) w i
```

Q2
caught, took, picked up

Q3
whispered, reply/answer, talking, asked, answer/reply, shouted, muttered

Pages 40-41 Ending a Story

Q1
At last the bus came.
The driver gave us all hot chocolate.

Q2
i) *Ending should include mention of cats or singing or friends. It should explain the noises.*
ii) *Ending should include something about Colin - eventually finding some nuts, or (from the picture) settling for pizza.*
iii) *Ending should be something like 'The unicorn gave them a ride home.'*

Pages 42-43 You Write a Story

Q1
Plan should have a begining, a middle and an end, as described on previous pages.

Q2
A good intro — setting the scene — who, when and where.
A good middle — something exciting happening.
A good ending — to round the story off with a happy, strange or unexpected occurence.

Section 5: Other Writing

Pages 44-45

Q1
i) one line, ii) big writing, iii) more about the writing

Q2
① *Anything that mentions fruit, veg, sweets or teeth.*
② *Anything to do with insects.*
③ *Something like 'Torquay' or 'South Devon' or holidays.*

Q3
Introduction should include something that tells the reader that the writing's about **insects — what they look like and where they live**.

Pages 46-47

Q1
General Information.
Ferret Behavior.
Looking After a Ferret.

Q2
Something like: How Hamsters Live
Something like: What They Eat

Q3
Anything suitable.

Pages 48-49 Bullet Points

Q1
There should be three circles — one around each dot.

Q2
There should be three MORE bullet points — one by each new sentence.

Q3
There should be two more sentences — one by each bullet point — each containing a fact from the text.

Q4
The bullet points are the important bit here — there should be two dots, each with a sentence by them.

Pages 50-51 Looking for Facts

Q1
George Stephenson, 1781, at evening classes, a coal mine

Q2
In 1814 Stephenson built his first steam locomotive. It could pull thirty tons of coal up a hill at 4mph. Over the next five years he built sixteen more engines.

Q3
Any two of: Horses were used to pull carts; Stephenson's was the first to use engines; his engines could do the work of fifty horses.

Q4
Either direct copies or reworded sentences from the text. Each sentence in the text is a seperate fact.

Pages 52-53 Endings

Q1
Yes; what you think; information writing, letters, stories

Q2
Elephants are... — Discovering Elephants
People's homes... — Inside a Victorian House
If you like... — Frog is a Hero — a Book Review

Q3
Following advice given, ending should say what writer thinks Florence did for people and why she was nice.

Pages 54-55 Practice Writing Exercise

Q:
Answer should have: a main title; a decent introduction; make use of bullet points and subheadings; state facts from the text and end in the writer's thoughts on the subject.

Pages 56-57 Writing a Letter

Q:
Letter should look like the example in overall appearance. The important bits are the start and the end. The middle should refer to what the camel said.

Answers